contents

JUST back from India, I first visited Cromarty in 1927. From Rosefarm my Middleton grandfather took my little sister Bright (who now owns and works the farm) and me to see the cottage where Hugh Miller, grandfather of his wife Lydia Davidson, had been born. Some memories of that visit have stayed with me – the chest or 'girnel' where the oatmeal was stored, the drawer for the cooled porridge and the bottom drawer for the latest baby; the fossils; and the fact that poor Hugh had been only five years old, my own age then, when his father was lost at sea. Grandfather told me that Hugh would take a slice of cold porridge in his pocket for the day. (Wrapped in what? Didn't it make his pocket messy?) And seeing my great-great-grandfather's statue on top of an immensely tall column – with a seagull sitting on his head.

Years later, on one of my regular visits to Rosefarm with my husband, we found the Miller genealogical tree had disappeared, so we set about reconstructing it. Hugh gave an account of his family in *My Schools and Schoolmasters*. References in it such as to his 'eldest maternal aunt' could be identified from the Old Parish Records. In the Public Record Office in London we found the crew lists of HMS *Centurion* and confirmed that the 'brother of [Hugh's] great uncle Alexander' was George who had indeed sailed round the world with Anson between 1740 and 1744 (one of the very few to survive the whole journey). From the Mackenzie family papers we discovered that Hugh's great-great-grandfather, James Mackenzie, 'the curate of Nigg', was descended from Kenneth Mackenzie, Prior of Beauly, who had refused

Avoch from E.

A Busy Corner, Cromarty

not to marry, defying the Pope and his bishop. This obduracy, displayed also by the curate's son-in-law, the dissenter Donald Roy, was a feature of Hugh's own character.

Census records, street directories, newspaper collections, Wills and school records were also searched to establish the background of Hugh's wife Lydia. Unfortunately most of her family papers had been destroyed by bombing during World War II, but we had a few letters and her own incomplete 'journal', which had been edited by her granddaughter and published in *Chambers' Journal*.

The Cottage visitors' book enabled me to contact other living descendants of the four children of Hugh and Lydia: Harriet, William, Bessie and Hugh. And in 2002, at the gathering in Cromarty to celebrate the 200th anniversary of Hugh's birth, we had 24 out of the then known 60 gathered at Rosefarm. They came from as far afield as the USA, Bangkok and Hong Kong. Others live in the UK, many still around the Cromarty and Moray Firths, and in France and Australia. All of us are grateful to the National Trust for Scotland for making it possible to have the Miller properties in Cromarty available to the public as a permanent memorial to Hugh and Lydia. I hope that many a young visitor will be inspired to be like Hugh and fill their lives with curiosity and achievement.

Marian McKenzie Johnston
London, 2005

Below: the old photographs show Cromarty scenes from the early twentieth century

HUGH MILLER'S BIRTHPLACE, CROMARTY.

Right: head armour of the fossil fish Coccosteus, *lettered by Hugh when he was working out the constituent parts of the skeleton*

Below: the manuscript of Hugh's book Scenes and Legends of the North of Scotland

Opposite page: Miller wearing his characteristic plaid, photographed in the 1840s

MORE of Hugh Miller's works are in print now than for nearly a century, yet he remains largely unread and his works, once familiar to tens of thousands throughout the world, are little known even in his native Scotland. Why? Some of his geology has proved flawed, as happened with the work of many another pioneer. His stand against evolutionary ideas soon became a lost cause – but he was writing before Darwin established the grounds for our modern understanding of the subject. And Hugh's writing style may seem on first acquaintance very dated.

Miller has not deserved this descent into obscurity. His fossil collection, including many original discoveries, was and remains of great importance to science, and the appeal of his writing is being rediscovered. James Robertson, the Scottish Parliament's first Writer-in-Residence, argues that rich rewards await those with enough patience to become familiar with Miller's Victorian modes of expression. He proved his point by helping to secure the republication in the 1990s of two of Miller's most accessible works, his autobiography, *My Schools and Schoolmasters*, and his folkloric masterpiece, *Scenes and Legends of the North of Scotland*.

Dr Robertson writes, in a contribution especially for this guidebook: 'The curious thing is how deeply Miller gets under the skin of those who do read him. They tend to develop a great enthusiasm for him as a personality, as a writer, and as a representative of the age in which he lived. His style may now seem old-fashioned, even at times long-winded – one could never describe Miller as a master of the sound-bite – but that is one of its virtues. He takes time to explain, to tell a story or to describe a fossil or a geological process, at a pace which obliges the reader to pay attention and gradually become absorbed. So much of what he had to say still rings with clarity, honesty and extraordinary vividness.'

This book presents a fresh review of the interconnecting themes in Hugh Miller's life. We hope that it will contribute to wider recognition for Miller as a worthy figure in the pantheon of great Scots.

A born story-teller

HUGH Miller was born in the building now called Hugh Miller's Birthplace Cottage, in Cromarty, on 10 October 1802. For him, it was a home steeped in Cromarty's history. His grandfather and father were seafarers, like his great-grandfather John Feddes, who built the Cottage.

Hugh would in later life write a long, gripping account, full of hero worship, of his father's adventures as a sailor. He followed this with tales of his Uncle Sandy's exploits in Nelson's Mediterranean fleet. He eagerly absorbed his mother's and his uncles' tales of family forebears, and borrowed every book he could from literate neighbours. He 'perused with avidity the voyages of Anson, Drake, and Raleigh,' volumes that formed only a small part of his 'library in a box of birch-bark'. By the age of eight, Hugh had read Homer's *Odyssey* and *Iliad* in translation.

When he had finished repeating the stories of Sinbad, Bluebeard, Aladdin and Robinson Crusoe to his schoolmates, Hugh went on to make up his own tall tales. So a teacher named him *Sennachie* (Gaelic for story-teller). The story of his own rascally, but magically adventurous, boyhood would in turn enter town lore.

However, Hugh's fortunes, and those of his family, were to take a sudden and permanent turn for the worse when his father perished in a shipwreck off Peterhead in November 1807. The mother, the boy, then just turned five, and his two older sisters were reduced to poverty. Hugh never got over his father's loss. For months he went on hoping in vain for the return of his father's sloop, with its distinctive 'two stripes of white and two square top-sails'.

Hugh went wild, played truant, stabbed a boy in the leg (in retaliation), led a gang roaming the South Sutor woods and caves, and quit school altogether at 15 after a brawl with a teacher. Thereafter, his books, the Sutor headlands and shorelines, the antiquities of the town, and his mentors became his 'schools'.

His maternal uncles James and Sandy Wright took him in hand. James the harness-maker was fond of a good joke, wise and, wrote Hugh, 'possessed more traditionary lore than any man I ever knew'. Serious-minded Sandy, the cartwright turned sawyer who knew more of nature than many a professor of natural history, showed him the life in 'every hole and cranny along several miles of rocky shore'.

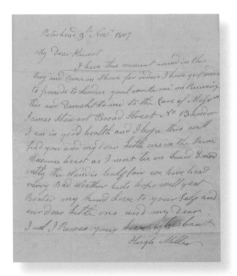

Top: the last letter Hugh's father wrote to his mother, shortly before he perished at sea. He hoped the weather would improve and passed on his love to his 'little ones'

Above: painting by an unknown artist, c1865, showing the Cottage (left), Miller House (now the Hugh Miller Museum) (centre) and Braefoot, the home of Lydia's mother (right)

Above: the Cottage kitchen with, from left: 'gossip' chair; yoke for carrying pails; spinning wheel; heather 'besom' (broom); kitchen range with 'swee', a movable iron bar for cooking meat over the fire; and wall-mounted bed-warming pan

Left: painting of the Cottage, possibly by Hugh's daughter Harriet. It is inscribed 'My father's birthplace ... with love Harriet'

Opposite page, clockwise from top left: Hugh's writing room; the top-floor room where Hugh feared meeting his great-grandfather's ghost; bedroom with (right) a birchbark box like the one where Hugh kept his first 'library'

The house became even sadder when his two older sisters both died of a 'deadly fever'. Hugh left home at the age of 17, when his mother remarried, although he often stayed there on return visits. He apprenticed himself as a stonemason with another uncle, David Williamson. Uncles James and Sandy had wished he would train for a profession, but Hugh believed mason-work would enable him to pursue his passions for literature and natural science.

'Humble as my apartment may seem, it is a place of some little experience in the affairs of both this world and the other'

'The low long house built by my great-grandfather the buccaneer'

While Hugh left us plenty of compelling accounts of his forebears and his own experiences, he recorded very little about the architectural history or the domestic life of the Cottage. He described only the room in which four generations of his family were born, which he turned into his writing room.

The cottage built by old Feddes was a large dwelling, at least by comparison with the typical 'little sod-covered cottage, with round moor stones sticking out of its mud walls' common in the district of Fishertown just across the road. Recent research by the Royal Commission on the Ancient and Historical Monuments of Scotland (RCAHMS) has shown that it may have begun life as a 'ha' house' – a house with a central hall open to the roof, and rooms and lofts at each end. Its 'hingin' lum' (canopied chimney), now in the reception area, originally occupied the site of the existing stair. This lum served as an indoor fish smokery, which also suggests wealth, since most smoking in those days was done in an outbuilding, or simply under an upturned boat. In a later phase of the building's life, just before Hugh's birth, it seems a floor was inserted into the open hall, effectively giving the whole edifice two storeys.

His mother remained in the Cottage until her death in 1864. In the next 25 years or so, it had a chequered history of occupation, and frequently fell into disrepair. Its flagstone floor, resting on bare earth, and its rubble-stone walls, clay-mortared, render it ineradicably damp. Its maintenance has been a demanding task ever since.

According to a report in the *Invergordon Times* of 22 June 1864, the family had 'given orders for its repair'. One letter of Miller's son William suggests it may have contained at some point a smithy. A part of it is believed to have been let to the Dorcas Society, a club of gentlewomen who sewed clothes for the poor.

What surely saved the building for posterity was the decision by Miller's youngest son, Hugh junior, in the late 1880s to establish it as a museum in his father's memory.

In 1926 family descendants passed administration of the Cottage to the Cromarty Town Council, while retaining ownership. In its turn, the Council found that 'the task of an overhaul might entail a rather heavy burden on local finance' and, in 1938, the family gifted it to the National Trust for Scotland. The Cottage was handed over at a great ceremony during which Miller's sundial-stone was presented by the Cromarty Provost's son, Dr Walter Johnstone. The sum of £500 was raised in a national appeal for preservation and restoration.

In the years of austerity, before, during, and after World War II, a local committee did its best to care for the building. It was rethatched in 1949. On the 150th anniversary of Miller's birth, in 1952, it was found to be, according to one newspaper report, 'rather a gloomy place', with a moss-laden, leaking roof, and another appeal raised £356 12s 7d for repairs. It was last rethatched in 1977. It has enjoyed two royal visits, by the Queen and Prince Philip on 25 June 1964, and Prince Charles on 30 September 1994.

The Cottage is now interpreted through an audio tour, in which visitors can hear Hugh's reminiscences, including the frightful 'severed hand' apparition on the night of his father's death; how he scratched down his tales of spectres in his 'writing room'; and how he painstakingly assembled the heaps of stony fins, spines and tails he had collected into their complete fossil forms, by the light of a candle or two and the fire.

The Trust has restored the Cottage as far as possible to its original status as the dwelling-place of the family. The audio tour takes you first round the grounds, including the cobbled Courtyard, and the Scottish Wild Garden planted in the 1990s to reflect Hugh's love of all the natural wonders in his environment.

Opposite page: the Cottage's Wild Garden

HUGH Miller was a stonemason for nearly 15 years, toiling for a pittance through the prime of his life, and to the near ruin of his health. He began as a journeyman mason, just one among the thousands of artisans who literally built the new Scotland that was emerging from the huge economic and social upheavals sweeping the country.

He was first employed in itinerant mason squads, carrying out works in the counties of Ross and Cromarty associated with agricultural improvement, such as new farm steadings, labourers' bothies, sheepfanks, and drystane dykes. Then he tried his luck 'among the stone-cutters of Edinburgh – perhaps the most skilful in the profession in the world'.

This page and opposite: calotypes of Edinburgh in the 1840s by David Octavius Hill and Robert Adamson showing a stone-cutting gang; the Scott Monument under construction; and Hugh Miller posing as a stonemason in the Calton Cemetery

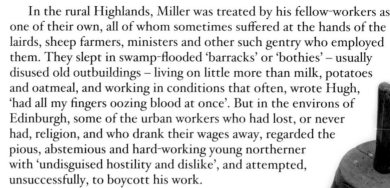

In the rural Highlands, Miller was treated by his fellow-workers as one of their own, all of whom sometimes suffered at the hands of the lairds, sheep farmers, ministers and other such gentry who employed them. They slept in swamp-flooded 'barracks' or 'bothies' – usually disused old outbuildings – living on little more than milk, potatoes and oatmeal, and working in conditions that often, wrote Hugh, 'had all my fingers oozing blood at once'. But in the environs of Edinburgh, some of the urban workers who had lost, or never had, religion, and who drank their wages away, regarded the pious, abstemious and hard-working young northerner with 'undisguised hostility and dislike', and attempted, unsuccessfully, to boycott his work.

However, Hugh's skill won him through every test. He 'acquired a very considerable mastery over the mallet' in less than a fortnight of starting his apprenticeship, 'hewing nearly two feet of pavement to his [master's] one'. At Niddrie, just south of Edinburgh, he was just as quick to pick up the most difficult fancy work – deeply moulded, long, slim mullions and transoms (window lintels).

The lungs of masons, exposed, like the colliers', to clouds of toxic dust, quickly became diseased, which at least partly explained some of the hard drinking. The disease – it may have been a form of either pulmonary tuberculosis, or silicosis – was then called simply the 'stone-cutter's malady', and the average life expectancy of a mason was 45. Miller's own health broke when he was only 23, and forced him to return to the north and undertake the much lighter trade of ornamental sculpture, in which he continued for another ten years.

In all this time, he wrote ceaselessly and explored the countryside in every spare moment. He recounts a telling exchange with 'Mad Bell', Isobel MacKenzie, while working by the River Conon. She asks him: 'What makes *you* work as a mason. You are merely in the disguise of a mason.' Intuitively, she understood that he was a young man of wide learning and high ambition. However, a genuine stonemason he was, and would remain proud of it all his days.

Above right: one of the mallets Hugh used for stone-cutting can be seen in the Museum

THE
CLEOPATRA
AS SHE SWEPT PAST
THE TOWN OF
CROMARTY
WAS GREETED
WITH THREE CHEERS
BY CROWDS OF
THE INHABITANTS
AND
THE EMIGRANTS
RETURNED
THE SALUTE
BUT
MINGLED WITH
THE DASH
OF THE WAVES
AND THE MURMURS
OF THE BREEZE
THEIR FAINT
HUZZAS SEEMED
RATHER SOUNDS
OF WAILING
AND
LAMENTATION
THAN OF A
CONGRATULATORY
FAREWELL

One of today's foremost letter-carvers, Richard Kindersley, inscribed this magnificent Caithness flagstone standing on Cromarty links, known as the Emigration Stone. It is a memorial to the thousands of emigrants who sailed from Cromarty for the New World in the 1830s and 1840s. It is also a tribute to Hugh Miller the stonemason and the writer – its inscription is taken from his eloquent report on the departure of the emigrant ship Cleopatra. *The stone was erected in 2002, the bicentenary of Miller's birth*

'TRADITION is a meteor, which if once it falls, cannot be rekindled.' *Dr Samuel Johnson*

Hugh Miller chose this quotation to begin his classic book of folklore, *Scenes and Legends of the North of Scotland*: it emphasised his conviction of the importance of preserving native folklore. Working on this collection in the 1820s, Hugh was following the first great recorders of tradition as it stood on the verge of oblivion, such as Robert Burns and Sir Walter Scott. Miller held both authors in the highest esteem. In one of his rare pieces of fiction, entitled *Recollections of Burns*, he cast himself as Matthew Lindsay, a sailor of Irvine, who befriends the poet and enjoys long philosophical conversations with him. And he recalled that, during his unhappy days as a mason working near Edinburgh, he 'had ... several times lingered in Castle Street of a Saturday evening, opposite the house of Sir Walter Scott, in the hope of catching a glimpse of that great writer and genial man, but had never been successful.'

As a youthful amateur antiquarian, Hugh amassed, mainly from his extended family and the older inhabitants of Cromarty, more than 350 traditional stories of ghosts, green ladies, witches, fairies, mermaids, smugglers, seers, hellfire preachers, wicked lairds and benefactors. He included his own encounters with the otherworldly. He traced the legends of holy wells, stormbound caves, ruined castles. He related deeds of Wallace, of Jacobins and Jacobites; he recorded recollections of rumbustious market days, and famine riots.

Albums with selections of his best stories are offered to visitors in the Cottage reading room. Here you might choose to share the second sight of Donald Roy, seer of Nigg; listen to the dreadful imprecations of the witch Stine Bheag of Tarbat; shiver at jockey Tam McKechan's disappearance, captured by the Eathie fairies; or laugh at Nannie Miller's

'… the rib-like bands, which project from the beach, [like]

portions of the skeleton of some huge antediluvian monster'

outwitting of two of the Bonnie Prince's marauding Highlanders.

Hugh got his first break as a writer when Robert Carruthers, the editor of the *Inverness Courier* (founded 1817), published some of these tales in a series, 'The Traditionary History of Cromarty'. Miller later expanded this into his first published prose work, *Scenes and Legends of the North of Scotland* (set principally in the counties of Ross and Cromarty). For several years, Hugh acted as the *Courier*'s Cromarty correspondent on contemporary events, covering emigration, shipwrecks, lodge parades, and cholera outbreaks – even episodes of witchcraft. The *Courier* also published for him, at his own expense, a 'slim volume' of poetry, *Poems in the Leisure Hours of a Journeyman Mason*, which Miller later admitted should have been committed to the fire. He was disappointed not to have made good as a poet.

Dr Lizanne Henderson, lecturer in history at the University of Glasgow, is one of several commentators who believe that Miller's role as a pioneering folklorist has been overlooked. In an essay in *Celebrating the Life and Times of Hugh Miller* (see 'Further reading'), she writes: 'His work has tremendous value not only since he was the first to record systematically the folklore of the North East region, nor simply because of the sheer volume of material he collected, but because he collected narratives from within the society from which they came.'

Dr Henderson has also noted the paradox of Miller's absorption with superstition and his intellectual rejection of it: 'Miller walked between two worlds. He was a country boy. But he was also an urban-dweller, searching for acceptance among the highly educated men and women with whom he mixed.' For them, accounts of the fey and the supernatural were acceptable only as quaint, whimsical survivals from a savage past

'My first, my only love'

Above: a modern copy by William Kay of an original portrait of Lydia by journeyman artist Grigor Urquhart

Below right: marriage bible, in which Hugh wrote verses for Lydia, 'my first, my only love, the kindest, dearest, best'

Opposite page: Hugh's desk at the Commercial Bank, and trunk for carrying money to Tain. The engraved plate records the presentation of the desk by the Bank to the Hugh Miller Institute (now the Cromarty Public Library) on the occasion of a lecture in January 1937 by former Prime Minister J Ramsay MacDonald

HUGH first became conscious of Lydia Mackenzie Falconer Fraser in the summer of 1831, just as he was finishing a day's hewing in his uncles' garden. He was 28 years old, she 19. He saw at once she was 'very pretty' and looked even younger than her age. He soon found he had been 'misled by the extreme youthfulness of her appearance, and a marked juvenility of manner', and that she had intellectual faculties of the first order. She in her turn found him 'a sort of dictionary of fact'. He began to fall in love with her, although without hope, because he knew she enjoyed the attentions of better-looking, younger men, with better prospects. But her heart had already been won by 'the Cromarty poet', as he was known, who, in her own words, had 'eyes the colouring of a deep blue, tinged with sapphire'.

When Lydia's widowed mother realised her daughter had fallen for a man who apparently had no prospects, she banned them from meeting alone. Hugh later told his sweetheart that he 'cut a notch in the beam which crossed the roof of his cottage for every day on which we had not met'. Eventually, the widow allowed an engagement. Hugh could not find a post in the professions that would make him a more eligible match, and the couple considered emigration to America. Then, in the winter of 1834, Hugh's friend Robert Ross, whose daughter Harriet was being taught at Lydia's 'little school', became the first agent for the Commercial Bank in Cromarty, and offered Hugh the post of accountant. He trained at Linlithgow, from where he sent Lydia a stream of love letters. They married at last on 7 January 1837 and, following a brief honeymoon in Elgin, moved immediately into their new home, now called Miller House and the site of the museum. Visitors can see here the marriage Bible that Hugh dedicated to 'my first, my only love'. The couple remained here until his departure for Edinburgh to edit *The Witness*, at the start of 1840.

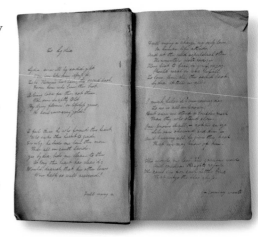

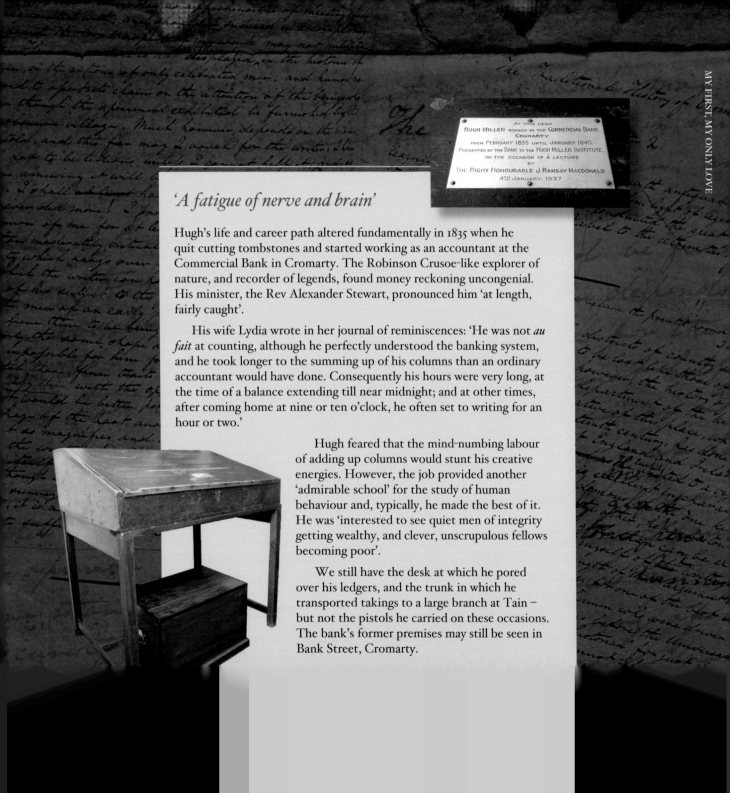

At this desk
HUGH MILLER worked in the COMMERCIAL BANK
CROMARTY
from FEBRUARY 1835 until JANUARY 1840.
Presented by the BANK to the HUGH MILLER INSTITUTE.
on the occasion of a lecture
by
THE RIGHT HONOURABLE J. RAMSAY MACDONALD
4th JANUARY, 1937.

'A fatigue of nerve and brain'

Hugh's life and career path altered fundamentally in 1835 when he quit cutting tombstones and started working as an accountant at the Commercial Bank in Cromarty. The Robinson Crusoe-like explorer of nature, and recorder of legends, found money reckoning uncongenial. His minister, the Rev Alexander Stewart, pronounced him 'at length, fairly caught'.

His wife Lydia wrote in her journal of reminiscences: 'He was not *au fait* at counting, although he perfectly understood the banking system, and he took longer to the summing up of his columns than an ordinary accountant would have done. Consequently his hours were very long, at the time of a balance extending till near midnight; and at other times, after coming home at nine or ten o'clock, he often set to writing for an hour or two.'

Hugh feared that the mind-numbing labour of adding up columns would stunt his creative energies. However, the job provided another 'admirable school' for the study of human behaviour and, typically, he made the best of it. He was 'interested to see quiet men of integrity getting wealthy, and clever, unscrupulous fellows becoming poor'.

We still have the desk at which he pored over his ledgers, and the trunk in which he transported takings to a large branch at Tain – but not the pistols he carried on these occasions. The bank's former premises may still be seen in Bank Street, Cromarty.

The family knew domestic harmony and tragedy in equal measure. Their first-born daughter Elizabeth (Liza), died of a fever aged only 17 months, in the spring of 1839. Their next daughter, Harriet, was born in November 1839. During these three short years, Miller contributed some of his most important discoveries to the new science of geology. He also composed the fiery polemic against patronage in the Church of Scotland, his *Letter to Lord Brougham* [the Lord Chancellor] *from One of the Scotch People*, which transformed the agitation for reform into a national public campaign.

The couple lived in what might be termed 'genteel poverty'. He earned a mere £60 a year as an accountant at the Commercial Bank. He supplemented his income by 'writing for the periodicals', and Lydia continued to teach a few pupils, so their combined income just about topped £100 a year.

Lydia's own reminiscences give a vivid insight into the conditions in which the couple lived: 'Our plenishing was not very great, but was "bien" and comfortable. We managed to furnish a parlour and bedroom and kitchen pretty well, and one of the attics had shelves put up for books and fossils. They were the nucleus of what afterwards became a large library and a fine museum. A table and chair were set there by the fire, and Hugh sometimes wrote or studied in it; but his times for study were now very rare ...

'Our ménage consisted for the first twelvemonth at least of but a single servant; but there was often to be seen in our kitchen an idiot lad named Foolish Angie, who had the strangest and strongest attachment to Hugh. If the latter happened to be across the ferry, as was now frequently the case on his bank journeys to Tain, Angus would watch for hours about the ferry-side to see if there was anything to carry or to accompany "Miller", as he called him, home in triumph.'

One of Lydia's pupils, Harriet Ross, later recalled: 'Miss Fraser was greatly looked up to by those she taught, and for myself in those days I almost worshipped her.

'My sisters and I and one or two other girls, went for four hours each day, save Saturday, to be taught by Mrs Miller ... Mr Miller generally returned from the bank before we left. He came home by the shore; and on the beach, especially if it were ebb tide, he never failed to pick up something which interested him; and when he joined us explained what he knew or conjectured about it ... And yet he had eaten nothing since breakfast time; but in truth dinner was not always in such a state of preparedness as might be desirable, for Mrs Miller had been occupied with her pupils, and the servant was careless. Most men would have been a little cross, but he most good-humouredly made jokes over failures and mistakes.

' "Come and take tea with us" was often said to me when school-hours were over, and I was well pleased to do this. Sometimes Mr Miller would sit and talk with his wife and with me; but oftener he wrote at a side table; and he always had a large Johnson's dictionary by him.'

Harriet also witnessed the Millers at worship in the East Church, drinking in the sermons of the Cromarty minister, the Reverend Alexander Stewart: 'I could not help noticing how intently Mr Miller listened to Mr Stewart's wonderful sermons, sometimes leaning on the table with a hand on each side of his head as if to shut out the sight of everyone but of him who was speaking to us.'

Hugh, Lydia and her young pupil Harriet particularly remembered 'happy holidays' on long Saturday afternoons and fine evenings, sailing round the Sutors in a little light yawl he had bought, catching fish for their supper. Hugh wrote of 'blue seas and purple hills and a sun-lit town in the distance, and tall wood-crested precipices near at hand, which flung lengthened shadows across shore and sea,' while Harriet saw 'the rays of the westering sun clothing each outstanding rock and pinnacle, and the trees in the hollows on the summit of the Sutor with a golden veil'; it was a scene of 'exquisite beauty which caused a hush in the soul'.

The fine Chinese export porcelain tea service in the parlour, dating from c1780, belonged to the Millers. Hugh's father may have acquired it second-hand, since it bears the initial 'G' which does not relate to any family member. Descendants are said to have taken the set to India and Australia and back, and it was evidently much prized, since almost every item has been repaired. It was gifted to the Museum by Hugh's great-great-granddaughter, Mrs Marian McKenzie Johnston

Left: William Bonnar's unfinished painting of Hugh and his eldest daughter Harriet

Opposite page, top: Hugh carved this headstone for his first-born daughter Elizabeth (Liza), who died of a fever aged only 17 months. It stands in the Old St Regulus churchyard, across the road from Cromarty House. The scalloped edges were a favourite motif of Hugh's

Bottom: Hugh and Lydia's four children, photographed c1861. From left to right, Hugh, William, Bessie and Harriet

Background: Cromarty, 'drawn on the spot' in 1824 by I Clark

21

MILLER HOUSE

The handsome Georgian-style house where Hugh and Lydia lived was completed in 1797 for Hugh Miller's sea-captain father, at a cost of £400. Shipmaster Miller had clearly done well in his coasting trade. However, that same year he lost his ship and all his capital in a storm. He was loaned enough money by a friend, and assisted by a sister, to purchase a new vessel, but he was compelled to rent out his 'more respectable' new dwelling, and remain in the old cottage built by his grandfather.

The master's villa was the first of a new style of houses built in Cromarty from the end of the eighteenth century. Cromarty's period of greatest prosperity, from around 1795 to 1830, began with improved agriculture and high prices for grain during the wars with revolutionary France, and continued from 1815 with a revived herring fishery. The harbour developed as an entrepot, an import/export base trading all round the coast of Britain, and with the ports of north-east Europe and the Baltic as far as St Petersburg.

Sea-captains and merchants quickly caught 'a rage for building' which would reflect their higher financial and social status. Among the finest shortly to follow Miller's villa were Bellevue and St Ann's, the merchants' mansions a few doors along Church Street to the east. These were all Georgian in their essential design; they also incorporated traditional Cromarty features such as steep-pitched roofs, crow-stepped gables, and 'cherry-pointing' – the reinforcing of joints with decorative small pieces of stone and slate.

Some of the sea-captain Miller's internal fixtures have survived intact, notably the fireplaces, staircase, and some of the doors, windows, shutters, and architraves. The central newel of the staircase may have been a ship's mast, sawn in half vertically. It was common for seafarers trading from Scottish east coast ports to use ship's timbers in their own homes.

The exterior structural masonry and detailed stonework have survived, although now covered with concrete-based harl. The house remained in the family's ownership until the National Trust for Scotland purchased it from a descendant in 1938 for £100. In 1971, the Trust undertook a full restoration under its Little Houses Improvement Scheme (LHIS), and sold it on for £12,000. When the now retired property manager Mrs Frieda Gostwick took up her post in 1992, she immediately realised the limitations imposed by the Cottage's lack of space and poor environmental conditions, and proposed the reacquisition of Miller House to establish a new museum. The building was reacquired for £55,000 in 1995, and the museum finally opened on 8 April 2004. One of the principal benefits has been to create the conditions for restoring to public display important Trust-held artefacts, some of which have been kept in storage for over 20 years, including Miller's plaids, his bank desk, and some letters and manuscripts. It has also facilitated donations and loans from other sources.

Conservation work has revealed fragments of information about the Millers' parlour. We know that a dado rail was removed, probably during the Greek Revival of the early nineteenth century. The bluish green and yellow of the wallpaper matches fragments of paint found in the room. In refurnishing the parlour to reflect the Millers' time, the Trust has been guided by recollections of the family and their visitors, and by surviving possessions in Thomas Carlyle's houses in Ecclefechan and Chelsea.

The fireplace is original: its simple detailing is of a type seen in the Baltic and Denmark. It has been painted white to imitate marble. The grate is also original to this house but possibly not to this room. Lydia may well have had a piano here for her pupils to play, though this square piano would have been a little old-fashioned by this time. The late eighteenth-century Pembroke table is placed centrally, as was customary: it has a reversible cover made by skilled damask weavers in Dunfermline.

LYDIA Fraser has only recently emerged from the shadow of her famous husband. One reason for her obscurity has been the loss in a World War II bombing in Brighton of a large quantity of family papers; another, that only one image of her survives. Fortunately this is a charming portrait of a young woman in love.

Lydia's mother, Elizabeth Macleod, was very proud of her Mackenzie descent, a pride which Lydia inherited. The family background of her father, William Fraser, is unknown. He died in 1828, not long after his business as an Inverness merchant failed. Lydia was a star pupil at Inverness Royal Academy, after which she continued her education as a boarder in the Princes Street, Edinburgh, home of George Thomson, where she attended classes in the arts and acquired the social graces. Thomson, by then elderly, was nationally celebrated as the collector and publisher of Robert Burns' songs. After William Fraser's death, his widow Elizabeth moved to Cromarty. Lydia joined her in 1830.

Lydia was one of the many well-educated women of the Victorian era who took up writing. She was an editorial assistant to Hugh in his early years at *The Witness*, contributing occasional book reviews, and helping him compose his leading articles. She was his intellectual equal and foil, fully in sympathy with the Free Church project, understanding his geological quest, and broadly sharing his views on public affairs. Her one novel, *Passages in the Life of an English Heiress* (1847), was an attempt to explain the Free Church's democratic and evangelical spirit to an English audience.

Above: detail of the copy of Lydia's portrait, painted in 1834 when she was 22

Below and opposite page: Lydia's popular books for children

Much more successful were her books for children, all but one published under the pseudonym Harriet Myrtle – possibly inspired by Hugh's comparison of her 'delicacy of myrtle' to his 'strength of the oak'. Lydia's best-seller was *Cats and Dogs, Nature's Warriors and God's Workers*, or *Mrs Myrtle's Lessons in Natural History*. The museum holds this work, and several others recently acquired, mainly from antiquarian booksellers in America. They are all attractively illustrated, and show why she was an adored teacher, but their Victorian moralistic sentimentality would not appeal to today's children.

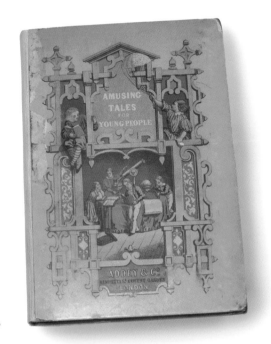

After Hugh's death, Lydia showed the depth of her dedication to him. Her first self-imposed task was to publish posthumously his *Testimony of the Rocks*, and to complete a seventh edition of *The Old Red Sandstone*. She sent copies of these to some of the most celebrated authors of the day, including Thomas Carlyle, Charles Dickens and John Ruskin, all of whom wrote back with high praises. Lydia went on to organise publication of five more volumes of Hugh's writings, mainly collections of articles previously serialised in *The Witness*, of which she wrote the prefaces to four. And she continued to write her children's books; she published some 17 in all.

Lydia was motivated not only by her love for Hugh but also by the need to support her family. There is no doubt the effort took a serious toll on her already fragile health. She moved restlessly from one spa to another, unsuccessfully seeking cures for her chronic back pains. Harriet, the older daughter, often undertook the burden of her care. Although seldom together for very long, Lydia and her children managed to maintain a fundamental family unity.

Sadly, late in life, Lydia publicly blamed Hugh's mother, Harriet, for his death, claiming that the 'overpowering terror' of the stories she told him in childhood returned to haunt him at the end. She passed away in 1876, aged 64, at the home of her daughter Bessie in Lochinver.

Coccosteis Cuspidatus
Head of animal. N.200th.

'THE SUPREME POET OF GEOLOGY'

'The supreme poet of geology'

THIS high accolade was bestowed on Hugh Miller by a scholar at the Bicentenary Conference in Cromarty in 2002, and makes a fitting title for the museum's centrepiece collection on its top floor. Dr Ralph O'Connor was placing Miller at the head of those who, from the 1820s onwards, throughout the nineteenth century, presented the Earth's history as a colossal spectacle to an enthralled mass public. Miller's word pictures of the Earth's path through time, informed by his faith in a 'Divine Hand', are among the most lyrical ever written. He was one of the great popularisers of what we call today earth sciences – he has been called the David Attenborough of his time. His articles in *The Witness* undoubtedly spurred thousands in all walks of life to go out 'geologising', and to begin to grasp the immensities of deep geological time.

Miller was one of the most wide-ranging fossil collectors of his day. He was interested not only in showing off complete and beautiful fossils in display cabinets, but in amassing evidence, even from the most insignificant fragments. He also exchanged, and in latter years even purchased, fossils to augment his collection. On his death, it numbered several thousand specimens. It was acquired in 1859 from his family for the nation for the sum of £1025 0s 6d. The collection remains one of the most important palaeontological holdings in the National Museums of Scotland (NMS), and is the source of several dozen specimens which NMS have kindly loaned for display at this museum.

Geology, although it was Hugh's favourite occupation all his adult life, was never his paid profession. He was elected president of the Royal Physical Society of Edinburgh in 1852, but did not gain the Professorship of Natural History at Edinburgh University when it fell vacant at around this time. According to an obituary in the *Illustrated London News*, he was known affectionately as 'Old Red' among some of his contemporaries, because of his acclaimed work in the Old Red Sandstone – perhaps also because he had hair colour to match!

Above: trilobite fossil

Left: reptile bones that Hugh found on the Isle of Eigg, as described in his book The Cruise of the Betsey

Opposite page, top: Hugh's hand-written label for a specimen of the Devonian fish Coccosteus

Opposite, bottom left: this solid silver medallion was made by Robert Crerar to celebrate the Miller bicentenary in 2002

Opposite, bottom right: Hugh used this geological hammer in his search for fossils

FOR THE GLORY OF GOD

For Miller, geology was not only a scientific pursuit, but a moral one. It was an 'improving' pastime, in which physical exercise combined with mental training. He was proud of his own physical prowess, and ability to walk 30 miles in a day. And, above all, geology served the greater glory of God. He enjoyed the beauty of fossils, which he said reflected their divine creation and God's love of beauty. Miller, like many Presbyterians, respected the evidence in the rocks. He despised the 'anti-geologists' who sought to insist on a literal reading of Genesis and deny the existence of geological time. He argued that Genesis was a religious vision of the sequence of geological time, rather than simply a myth of creation, but this notion was not very successful and is now largely forgotten.

The 1840s and 1850s were a time of great debate over early evolutionary notions. Miller could not accept them, for he especially insisted that humans were created separately from animals, rather than having evolved from them, because he held that humans had immortal souls and the accompanying moral responsibility, but animals did not. Miller engaged with those whom he called the 'infidel' evolutionists, and sought evidence to refute their contentions, with some success given the weakness of these early evolutionary concepts. However, the debate was rendered obsolete, some three years after Miller's death, by Charles Darwin's new (and very different) presentation of modern ideas of evolution by the mechanism of natural selection in his book, *On the Origin of Species* (1859).

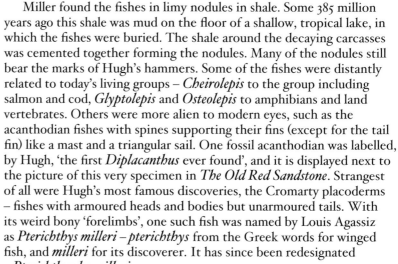

INTO 'THE OLD RED'

Miller's most famous geological book is undoubtedly *The Old Red Sandstone*, published in 1841. His discoveries of fossil fish in the Devonian deposits of Cromarty, and his descriptions of them, were acclaimed by some of the leading earth scientists of the day, including Charles Lyell, Sir Roderick Murchison and Louis Agassiz. In the next 60 years, this book went through many reprints, and was often used as a guidebook to local geology.

Miller found the fishes in limy nodules in shale. Some 385 million years ago this shale was mud on the floor of a shallow, tropical lake, in which the fishes were buried. The shale around the decaying carcasses was cemented together forming the nodules. Many of the nodules still bear the marks of Hugh's hammers. Some of the fishes were distantly related to today's living groups – *Cheirolepis* to the group including salmon and cod, *Glyptolepis* and *Osteolepis* to amphibians and land vertebrates. Others were more alien to modern eyes, such as the acanthodian fishes with spines supporting their fins (except for the tail fin) like a mast and a triangular sail. One fossil acanthodian was labelled, by Hugh, 'the first *Diplacanthus* ever found', and it is displayed next to the picture of this very specimen in *The Old Red Sandstone*. Strangest of all were Hugh's most famous discoveries, the Cromarty placoderms – fishes with armoured heads and bodies but unarmoured tails. With its weird bony 'forelimbs', one such fish was named by Louis Agassiz as *Pterichthys milleri* – *pterichthys* from the Greek words for winged fish, and *milleri* for its discoverer. It has since been redesignated *Pterichthyodes milleri*.

Miller tried to work out the very complex anatomies of these fishes for himself. It was difficult, because the fossil fishes of the Old Red Sandstone formation at Cromarty are often squashed, damaged and incomplete. He deliberately collected, rather than discarded, fragments, to help him reconstruct the complete fossil, and thence the complete living animal, in his mind, and on the written page. The reconstructions he drew himself and published in the book are not perfect by modern standards, but very good for the time. If you look at the *Coccosteus* in the display – another fish discovered by Miller – you can still see the letters Hugh painted on the individual plates of its bony armour, while trying to sort them out.

Miller had first got the collecting bug while still a teenager, some three miles away on the Moray Firth coast around Eathie, on the other side of the South Sutor headland. The rocks there are now known to be of Late Jurassic age, laid down just over 150 million years ago, although Miller like others placed them in the 'Lias' (Early Jurassic). Amongst the finds that most excited him in his 'marvellous library of Scotch Lias' were marine molluscs (shellfish) such as clams, ammonites (spiral-shelled extinct relatives of the modern pearly nautilus and octopus), and squid-like belemnites. Miller was told by a fellow stonemason how the solid, bullet-shaped ends of the internal skeletons of belemnites had been regarded traditionally as thunderbolts and were once sought out for the cure of sick cattle! But perhaps more important in the long run were his finds of fossil plants from Eathie and elsewhere on the north-east coast of Scotland, which, long after his death, continue to draw scientific attention. The exhibition here includes the actual specimen of a fossil fern from Helmsdale in Sutherland, used for an illustration in Hugh's last book, *Testimony of the Rocks*.

'Let me qualify myself to stand as interpreter between nature and the public'

Opposite page, top left: a life reconstruction drawing by Hugh of 'Pterichthys milleri' with modern model, top right

Opposite, middle: branch of a coniferous tree from the Jurassic at Eathie

Opposite, bottom: fossil fish Osteolepis *from the Old Red Sandstone at Cromarty*

This page, below: Miller the fossil detective at work. Left, the head armour of a large placoderm fish; centre, his plaster cast of it, painted to demarcate the different bony elements (Hugh's children spotted 'an angel, robed and winged' in this fish); right, an illustration, based on this specimen, in his book Footprints of the Creator

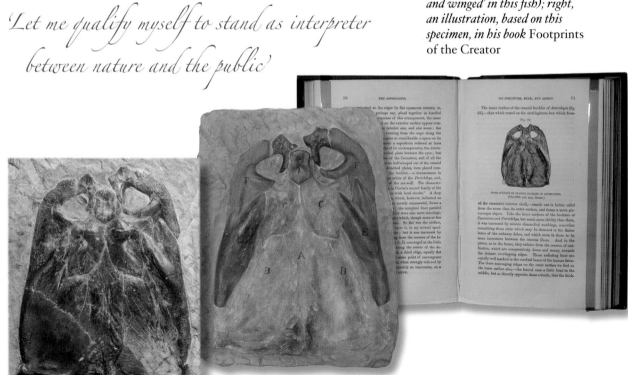

Two of his most readable books, published as one volume, *The Cruise of the Betsey* and *Rambles of a Geologist*, describe his 'rambles' while on summer holidays from *The Witness*. Hugh sailed on the *Betsey* with his old boyhood friend, the Rev John Swanson, who was now Free Church Minister for the Small Isles of Inverness-shire. Swanson had to minister to his congregation from this leaky old yacht, since the local landowners refused him a useable site on which to build a manse.

The boat nearly sank under them. Hugh had a wonderful time exploring the islands, discovering fossil plesiosaurs (extinct marine reptiles roughly equivalent to sea lions) and shellfish, and was intrigued by the ancient lava forming the striking hill of An Sgùrr on Eigg.

Hugh explored quarries and beaches all over Scotland, from Girvan to Portsoy, and from Orkney to Dumfriesshire, and the display shows a range of specimens from many of these locations. Occasionally he went further afield, to England, amongst other things to see how English fossils compared with Scottish finds of the same age, as he recorded in *First Impressions of England and its People*. Miller particularly enjoyed Dudley in the West Midlands where, in a quarry, fossils 'lay as thickly around me as ... shells and corals on a tropical beach'. He also admired the industriousness of English workers, and commented favourably on some of the womenfolk!

Hugh's collection naturally included many specimens from the Edinburgh area, such as fossil plants and other finds from the swampy forests of Carboniferous times whose remains formed the coal and ironstone so important to Scottish industry at the time, as he reported in his books *Edinburgh and its Neighbourhood* and *Sketch-book of Popular Geology*. There were also far more geologically recent fossils to be found, proof that Miller's Portobello home was built on what had previously been the sea floor! The sea level was much higher during the Ice Ages. On display is a clam that once lived in brackish water, in an estuary that is now dry land: it was found in a claypit near where Miller lived.

The Miller collection is fascinating, first because of its scientific importance, which makes it the subject of ongoing research, especially on its 'type specimens'. (A type specimen provides the foundation for naming fossil species and sometimes genera (groupings of species).) The collection also has great historical and cultural value. Like famous paintings, poems and buildings, Hugh's fossils entered the Victorian consciousness: his drawings of them and his depictions of vast changes, movements and transformations gave many their first understanding of the Earth's great age and its process of development, and led readers from there to what the fossils might mean for one's view of life, the universe and creation.

In *Rambles*, Hugh gives his best description of himself in the field, dressed in 'a fatigue suit of russet. ...My hammer-shaft projected from my pocket; a knapsack with a few changes of linen slung suspended from my shoulders; a strong cotton umbrella occupied my better hand; and a gray maud [plaid], buckled shepherd fashion aslant the chest, completed my equipment.'

Above: sculptor Nicholas Kidd's depiction in Portland Stone of Miller's 'winged fish' (Pterichthyodes milleri)

Opposite page, top: one of Miller's fine drawings, this time of Coccosteus

Bottom: belemnite (left) and ammonite, both from the Jurassic deposits at Eathie

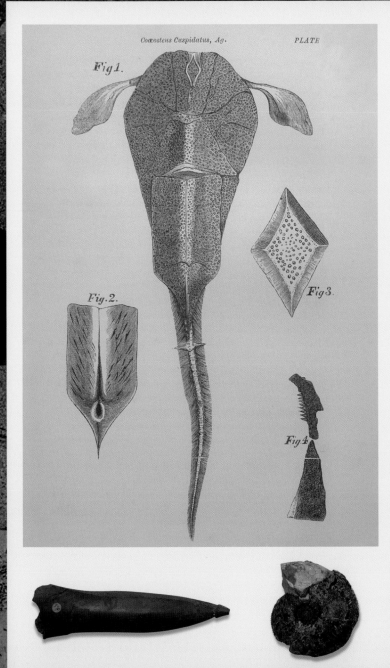

Cocosteus Cuspidatus, Ag.   PLATE

Fig 1.

Fig.2.

Fig 3.

Fig 4.

FOSSIL DISPLAYS AT CROMARTY

Hugh Miller's younger son, Hugh junior (1850-96), followed in his father's footsteps in becoming a geologist. In the mid-1880s, he was employed by HM Geological Survey in mapping, at his own request, the same Cromarty terrain made famous by his father some 40 years earlier. He took the opportunity to set up a museum, possibly initially in this building. It was situated for 114 years in the birthplace Cottage. The first visitors' book indicates an official opening date of 20 May 1890. The exhibitions included bird skins, bones and books on natural science, mingled with assorted fossils from various collections, and a large quantity of Miller's letters and manuscripts.

These were comprehensively reorganised in 1953, principally by Dr Charles Waterston, of the then Department of Geology in the Royal Scottish Museum (now NMS), on the basis that the tiny rooms were hopelessly overcrowded and 'the presentation lacked the necessary selection and classification'. Dr Waterston rearranged the fossils to illustrate Miller's best-known books on geology.

A second reorganisation in 1983 again aimed at improving access and the clarity of the presentation. The recent creation of a new museum at Miller House is described on p23.

The truth I speak

IN his early twenties, Hugh's boyhood friend the Rev John Swanson led him toward the evangelical Christian faith, which was to lie at the heart of everything he thought and did for the rest of his life.

In those days religious faith was at the core of life for the vast majority of the Scottish people. Yet when Hugh Miller took up his pen to write his *Letter to Lord Brougham* in 1839, he was addressing the Lord Chancellor with a plea to resolve a crisis, which he described as 'the decay of religion'. He believed that the power given by the 1712 Patronage Act to landowners to appoint ministers of their own choosing was an abuse, 'a deep and dangerous conspiracy against the liberties of our country'. Complacent ministers had brought about widespread apathy and neglect. The lairds who, by land-ownership and rack-renting, exercised absolute power over their tenants, were also lording it over their people's souls. Speaking for the so-called Evangelical wing of the Church, Miller wanted the Kirk to return to the principles of John Knox and the Covenanters, in which Christ was acknowledged as head of the Church, and congregations had the right to elect their own ministers.

There were two parties in the Kirk – the Moderates, who wished to remain compliant with State control, and the Evangelicals. In one court case after another, the Patronage Act was upheld, and ministers were again 'intruded', or imposed, on congregations who did not want them. Hugh's *Letter* did not change the Lord Chancellor's mind, but, when published as a mass circulation pamphlet, it did help to rouse a nationwide popular movement in support of the Evangelicals' cause. And it led directly to the leading clergymen of that party inviting him down to Edinburgh to edit their new paper, *The Witness*.

Hugh took the editor's chair at the office of *The Witness* at 297 High Street, Edinburgh, on a January morning in 1840, well aware that the paper's cause was one opposed by the British state, the great lords of Parliament, the land and the law, and the majority of Moderates who ran the church, not to mention the rest of the press.

He immediately signalled the defiant stance of *The Witness* by placing a declaration by Knox on the paper's masthead: 'I am in the place where I am demanded of conscience to speak the truth, and therefore the truth I speak, impugn it who so list [whoever chooses to oppose it].'

His powerful leading articles denouncing the continuing cases of intrusion were a major factor in bringing matters to a head. The great schism finally erupted in 1843, when 474 ministers, out of a total of 1,195, walked out of the annual General Assembly of the Established Church, and founded the Free Church of Scotland. They sacrificed their livings, kirks and manses. Many lairds retaliated by refusing sites on which to build new churches, but in a few years Free Church congregations funded and erected over 730 places of worship for themselves.

Although the Free Church congregations restored the election of ministers, and set up schools and missions all over the British Empire, Miller regretted the schism. He would have much preferred the Established Church to have reformed itself from within. Eventually, long after his death, patronage was abolished in the Church of Scotland too.

Below, left: 'Could I do nothing for my Church in her hour of peril?' Hugh asked himself. His response was the fiercely polemical 'Letter to Lord Brougham from one of the Scotch People', which helped to change the course of church history

Below, right and background: Cromarty's historic East Church, one of hundreds to lose most of its congregation to the new Free Church as a result of The Disruption

Opposite page: detail showing Hugh Miller from D O Hill's 1866 painting of the Signing of the Deed of Demission of the Free Church of Scotland in 1843

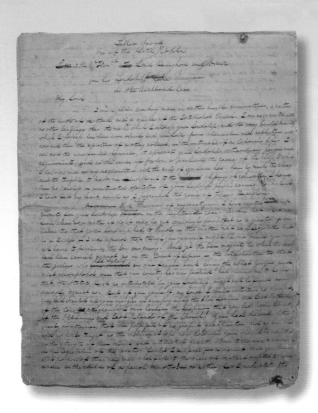

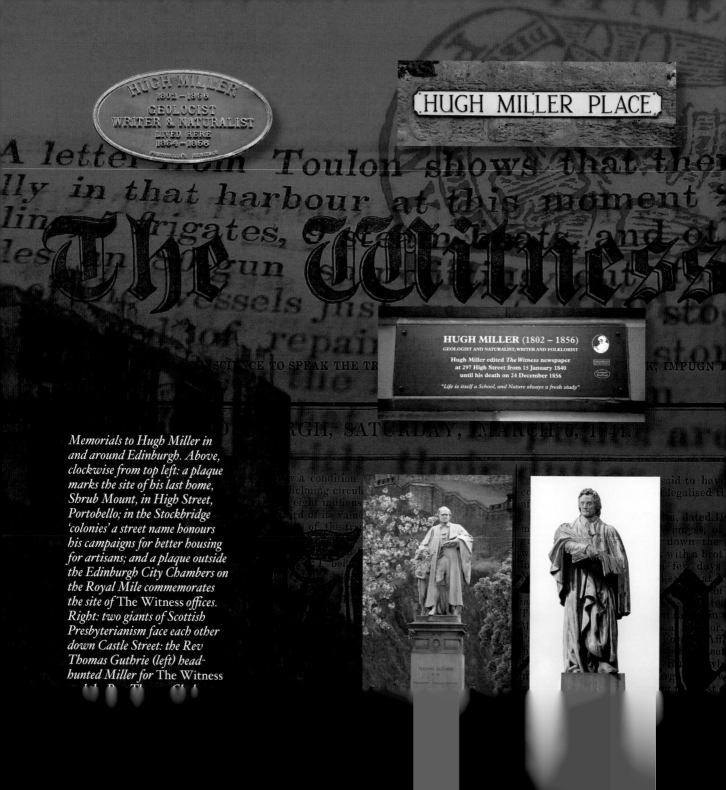

HUGH MILLER
1802–1856
GEOLOGIST
WRITER & NATURALIST
LIVED HERE
1854–1856

HUGH MILLER PLACE

HUGH MILLER (1802 – 1856)
GEOLOGIST AND NATURALIST, WRITER AND FOLKLORIST

Hugh Miller edited *The Witness* newspaper
at 297 High Street from 15 January 1840
until his death on 24 December 1856

"Life is itself a School, and Nature always a fresh study"

Memorials to Hugh Miller in and around Edinburgh. Above, clockwise from top left: a plaque marks the site of his last home, Shrub Mount, in High Street, Portobello; in the Stockbridge 'colonies' a street name honours his campaigns for better housing for artisans; and a plaque outside the Edinburgh City Chambers on the Royal Mile commemorates the site of The Witness *offices. Right: two giants of Scottish Presbyterianism face each other down Castle Street: the Rev Thomas Guthrie (left) head-hunted Miller for* The Witness*...*

Miller's support for the Free Church was, however, conditional. He rigorously maintained his paper's editorial independence of both dictatorial clergymen and the Whig government they supported. His outspoken criticisms led to an attempt by some leading ministers to oust him from the editorship. They complained of his 'want of delicacy, taste and tact', but his views were the real issue. Miller won the dispute and continued to edit the paper until his death.

Readers responded not only to his passionate denunciations of intrusion, but also to his campaigning journalism on many other issues of the day. He fought for better sanitation in the slums, for improved working conditions for agricultural labourers, and for non-denominational education. He lambasted the clan chiefs and lairds who cleared the glens of people for the sake of sheep and hunting estates. He called the almost entire depopulation of Rum an 'extermination' and said the degradation of the victims constituted the country's 'weakness and its shame'. In 'Sutherland As It Was and Is' he described the Sutherland Clearances of 15,000 souls over a period of nine years, to make way for sheep, as 'a fatal experiment' that ruined the country. He likened the experiment to 'dissecting a dog alive for the benefit of science'. It was, he said, carried out with 'atrocities unexampled in Britain for at least a century'. As he strode about the streets of Edinburgh, still wearing his shepherd's plaid, Miller was recognised by everyone as the self-taught 'lad o' pairts' who had come to be regarded as a people's champion. However, his concerns were humanitarian rather than politically motivated: he distrusted the 'Chartist agitators' and opposed their demand for universal suffrage.

Many of Miller's articles, for example those on land use and access, still resonate today, as do his comments on the follies and evils of imperial wars. Here is Miller on 'Conclusion of the War in Affghanistan' from *The Witness*, 3 December 1842 (Afghan insurgents had slaughtered a British army retreating from Kabul almost to the last man). 'War is an evil in all circumstances. It is a great evil even when just ... But it is peculiarly an evil when palpably not a just war ...'

Not surprisingly, some of Miller's articles aroused anger in influential quarters. But he proved the soundness of his editorship by making *The Witness* the second biggest-selling newspaper in the country after *The Scotsman*. He produced the twice-weekly paper for 16 years, in more than 1,500 editions, in which he wrote most of the leading articles and many of the reports. His success came at a heavy price, however, for his Free Church opponents cut off all contact with him. And the prolonged overwork broke his health.

Below: a family being evicted from their home in Argyllshire c1850. Miller's articles in The Witness *passionately denounced the Highland Clearances*

'THE ANCIENT INHABITANTS WERE CLEARED OFF, IN THE FIRST PROCESS, TO MAKE WAY FOR SHEEP; AND NOW THE PEOPLE OF SCOTLAND GENERALLY ARE TO BE SHUT OUT FROM THESE VAST TRACTS, LEST THEY SHOULD DISTURB THE GAME'

Professor Donald Macleod, Principal of the Free Church College, writes:

Over 40 years have passed since I found a copy of *My Schools and Schoolmasters* among a pile of old books in a Highland church hall. I still have it, stained, battered and heavily underlined, plus two other editions in reserve as well as a complete, though far from uniform, set of Miller's works.

They have influenced me profoundly, not least in my churchmanship. Miller's struggles against patronage were no abstract thing. He was fighting for a vision of the church. The struggle for 'the rights of the Christian people' was not merely a struggle against landlords. It was also, implicitly, a struggle against the clergy, who too often identified the church with themselves. Miller drove home the truth that the pews were not only served by the church: they were the church. If the people left, the church left.

He also knew that these same people, the people of Scotland's Presbyterian soil, demanded a learned ministry. He feared those who wanted to pepper the land with second-rate theological colleges rather than establish one centre of excellence; and he wearied of those young ministers who sustained themselves with the mantra, 'Preaching is but a small part of the duties of a minister.' If you filled the pulpits with such men, he said ('fine bodies', but poor preachers), they would soon empty the churches.

Linked to that was Miller's fear of the church going to war with science. That was a war she could never win. No scientific question could be settled by dogma. It could be settled only by the facts and these could be ascertained only by experiment and observation. More than any other single figure, Hugh Miller saved the church in Scotland from the obscurantism of Creation Science.

He also ensured that the churches had a social voice as well as a social conscience. Such essays as 'The Bothy System', 'The Cottages of our Hinds' and 'Sutherland As It Was and Is' combine brilliant description with searing anger and would be enough by themselves to launch a whole theology of liberation.

But Miller was more than an 'improving' writer. He was an entertainer, living by his own maxim that the first duty of a book was to be interesting and fully aware that if it lacked that quality no other attribute could make up for it. Profit (and even historical source-material) there may be in such volumes as *Scenes and Legends, First Impressions of England and its People*, and *The Cruise of the Betsey*. But first and foremost they are pure entertainment: prose windows, which not only reveal but enhance lost worlds.

Even in his dying he was an inspiration: a reminder that desperation is not damnation and that a soul may commit itself to divine mercy even in the moment of self-destruction.

Medal commemorating The Disruption. The front (right) contains significant dates in the history of Scottish Presbyterianism, and depicts the gravestones of leading clergymen. The reverse (far right) explains how 474 ministers resigned their livings in the Church of Scotland, because it was subject to 'the coercive interference of the civil courts'

*Above: David Octavius Hill's painting of ministers queuing
up to sign the Act of Separation and Deed of Demission, which
effectively set up the Free Church of Scotland. It hangs in the
Presbytery Hall of the Free Church on The Mound in Edinburgh*

*Top: a copy of the deed has been gifted to the Hugh Miller Museum
by Richard Beeching, a descendant of one of the signatories*

PHOTOGRAPHY – A NEW ART FORM

*Dr Sara Stevenson, Chief Curator of Photography,
Scottish National Portrait Gallery, writes:*

Both Hugh Miller and David Octavius Hill were
passionate Free Churchmen. Hill intended to paint
a grand historical painting of the Church's first
General Assembly. There was, however, an elementary
problem. After a few weeks, the hundreds of ministers
and elders would scatter to their homes across
Scotland; how then could he paint them? Sir David
Brewster, the distinguished physicist at the University
of St Andrews, persuaded Hill to meet Robert
Adamson, newly-established as a photographer, in a
sunny garden on Calton Hill in Edinburgh.

Adamson practised the 'calotype' process, invented
by William Henry Fox Talbot, which was the first
negative/positive process of photography, using good
drawing paper for both negative and positive and
printed by the sun itself. Hill and Adamson tried out
the new art with groups of the ministers as models,
and were astonished. These were not dry records or
pale sketches – they caught a sense of life in the light-
sensitive chemistry. By July 1843, Hill and Adamson
had found their work in photography so rewarding
that they entered into partnership to try what else they
could do.

One of the first of many to visit Hill and
Adamson's studio and have his portrait taken
was Hugh Miller. He appears in at least eleven
photographs, including a number of studies for the
painting. Hill and Adamson then carried the camera
over the road to the Calton cemetery, where they
made a more complete picture, showing Miller as a
stonemason leaning against a gravestone – the man
of action but also, in Miller's terms, the serious man,
meditating on death.

Hill was sociable, and it is evident from the
comparatively relaxed nature of the calotypes – which
might take two or three minutes' exposure – that he
and Miller would have been talking. Miller was so
interested that he wrote one of the first critical articles
on photography for *The Witness* in July 1843. In it he
enthusiastically discusses perspective, perception, the
construction of groups and the process's potential for
book illustration.

Hill and Adamson's calotype partnership took
over 3,000 photographs but lasted only four years,
ending in January 1848, with the tragically early
death of Robert Adamson. Hill and Miller remained
friends, and Miller is said to have kept a photograph,
perhaps the one of him as a stonemason, on his desk
to keep himself humble.

Hill's grand Free Church painting (opposite)
was not finished until 1866. It contains over 400
recognisable portraits, and the figure of Hugh Miller
is placed in a striking and prominent position in the
foreground. Hill wrote:

'The plaided form ... taking notes near the Clerks'
table, is the editor of the Witness newspaper ... a
name very dear to Scotland, and admired wherever
the English language is read – whose figure does not
bulk more prominently in the picture than did his
remarkable writings in the controversy involving the
Disruption, of which it may be said emphatically he
was one of the greatest leaders.'

*David Octavius Hill: a calotype from the Hill &
Adamson collection in the Scottish National Portrait
Gallery, Edinburgh*

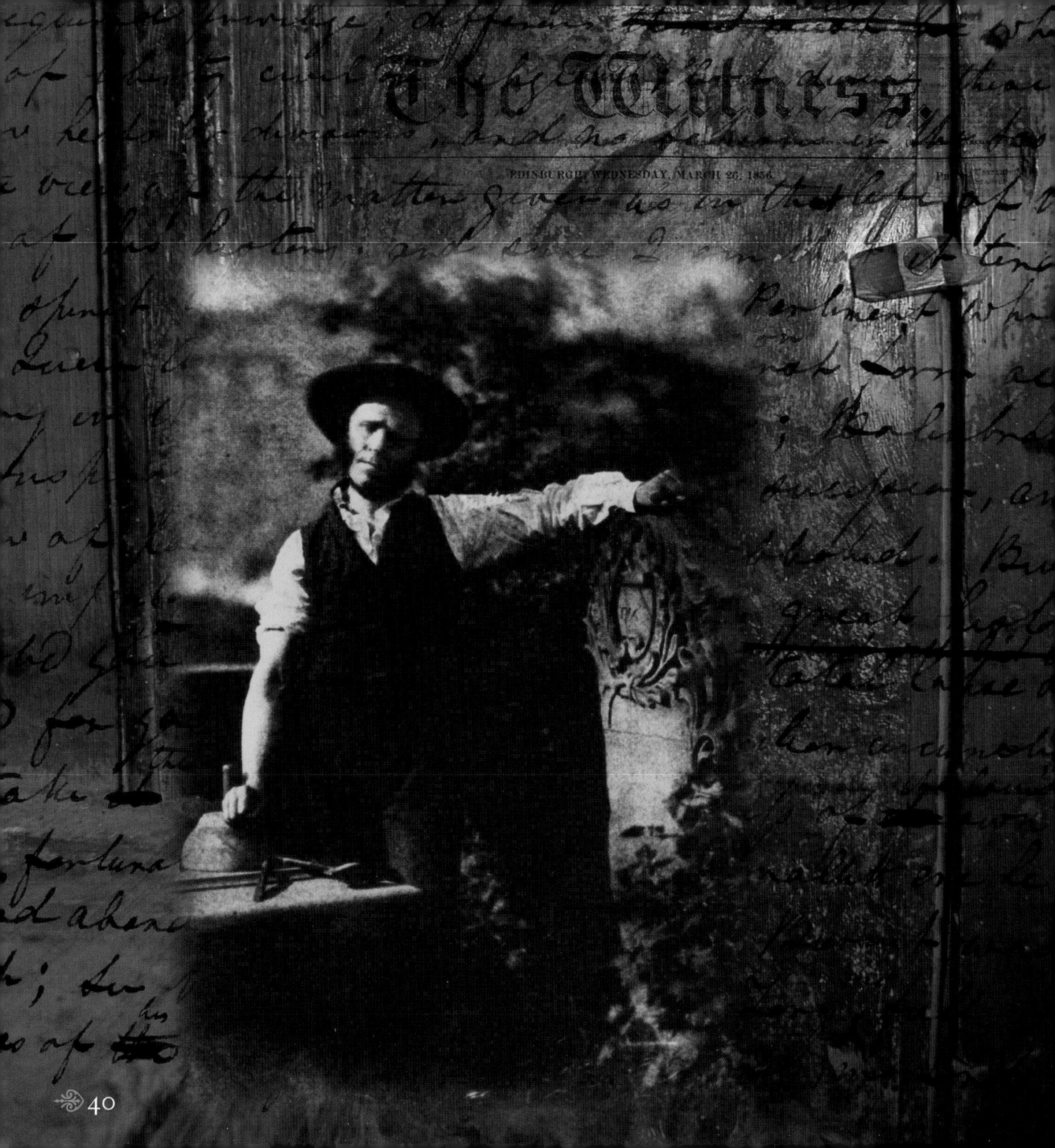
The Witness.
EDINBURGH, WEDNESDAY, MARCH 26, 1856.

'My brain is giving way'

MILLER carried pistols to defend himself against the armed robbers then infesting the streets of Edinburgh, because he often went fossil collecting, and walked home late at night, over quiet and unfrequented areas. He also kept the weapons under his pillow. He was terrified in case his matchless fossil collection would be burgled.

He killed himself by a single pistol shot discharged into the left side of his chest, in the early hours of Christmas Eve, 1856. The four doctors who conducted the post mortem found 'diseased appearances' in the brain, but the disease was not specified. They declared he had acted 'under an impulse of insanity'. That judgement permitted a Christian burial, and thousands lined the streets of Edinburgh as his funeral cortège made its way to The Grange Cemetery, where he was buried close to his mentor, Thomas Chalmers, the Free Church's first Moderator, and joined 20 years later by his wife.

The causes of Miller's suicide have been debated ever since. His ill-health had forced him to give up the public lectures he delivered to huge audiences. He had always been morbid, and became especially melancholy when his health gave way. He was exhausted with the overwork at *The Witness*. In his final days he suffered blackouts, and intense head pains which he described 'as if a very fine poignard had been suddenly passed through my brain'. Some commentators have suggested he was driven to it by unresolved tensions between his faith and science, but this has been discounted as 'utterly baseless' by Professor Macleod. The disease mentioned in the post mortem may have been a brain tumour, which could account for the blackouts and head pains.

Worse still were his nightmares of being pursued by witches and demons. He told one of the doctors the day before his death: 'My brain is giving way. I have had a dreadful night of it. I cannot face another such.' These remarks suggest that he felt himself becoming possessed by evil, and feared imminent madness. A man of his faith, and intellect, could not bear that. He was alone, Lydia sleeping downstairs because of her bad back.

His suicide note (to the right), although semi-incoherent, sums it all up.

Model of Miller's death mask

Dearest Lydia,
My brain burns. I must have walked; and a fearful dream rises upon me. I cannot bear the horrible thought. God and Father of the Lord Jesus Christ, have mercy upon me. Dearest Lydia, dear children, farewell. My brain burns as the recollection grows.

My dear, dear wife, farewell.

HUGH MILLER

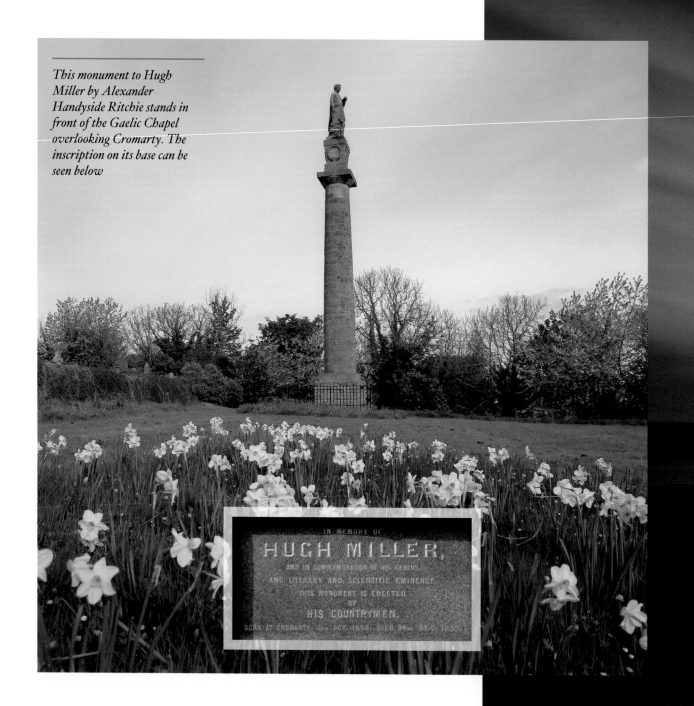

This monument to Hugh Miller by Alexander Handyside Ritchie stands in front of the Gaelic Chapel overlooking Cromarty. The inscription on its base can be seen below

IN MEMORY OF

HUGH MILLER,

AND IN COMMEMORATION OF HIS GENIUS,
AND LITERARY AND SCIENTIFIC EMINENCE,
THIS MONUMENT IS ERECTED
BY
HIS COUNTRYMEN.

BORN AT CROMARTY 10th OCT. 1802. DIED 24th DEC. 1856.

It is not surprising that much analysis of Miller's psyche has focused on such a sad and terrible end. Dramatic productions, including an opera and a play, have also taken the death as a starting point. However, it is a mistake to lay too much emphasis on Miller's death; his achievements in life are what matter. His statue, erected by public subscription in 1859, only three years after his death, looks out to the North and South Sutor headlands and the scene of his greatest discoveries.

An engraving by Bell from a photograph by J G Tunny of Hugh reading, 'one of the most delightful of my amusements'

'Life itself is a school, and Nature always a fresh study'

THE creation of a secure archive room in the museum has enabled the Trust to store valuable original manuscripts and other artefacts on the premises; to rotate the contents of our displays; and to accept new items of 'Milleriana' as they are donated. We welcome offers of relevant material, specifically connected to Miller; acceptance is subject to the Trust's acquisition policy.

Among the items held in the archive room are handsomely bound volumes of *The Witness*; some manuscripts; a copy of the Free Church Deed of Demission; early editions of Miller's collected works; the surviving books of his personal library; and visitors' books. Many fossil specimens which featured in the Cottage's geology exhibition are also stored there.

In the Cottage reading room, we have a secure bookcase housing a collection of over 150 titles, including those on the 'Further reading' list, and other works on geology, natural, social and local history, folklore, church matters and letter-cutting. A full list can be found on the website www.hughmiller.org. Visitors can ask staff to remove any book from the case if they would like to look at it on site.

The Miller Cromarty properties are designed to provide opportunities for further study of his life, work and period, supporting the invaluable reference material in the national collections in Edinburgh. They are intended also to serve as an educational resource, providing access to their heritage for people of all ages living in the Highlands. Group visits are welcome from schools, field clubs, colleges and universities anywhere in the country.

Above and opposite: pupils from Cromarty Primary School enjoying the Hugh Miller Museum

The Hugh Miller Trail

On the Eathie foreshore, an excellent outdoor interpretation facility is housed in a former salmon-fishing bothy which has been restored for the purpose by Cromarty Arts Trust. A panel explains Miller's fieldwork there. The Arts Trust has also placed highly informative panels on the Cromarty Links, and at the foot of the South Sutor.

The national collections and other sites of interest in Edinburgh

The Trust has placed a large quantity of Miller papers on deposit in the National Library of Scotland (NLS), George IV Bridge. The NLS and the Free Church College, 15 North Bank Street, The Mound, have complete sets of *The Witness*. Miller's hand-written Letter Book of over 900 pages is held by the New College Library of Edinburgh University in Mound Place. Hugh Miller's fossil collecton is held by the National Museums of Scotland. At the time of writing, there is a special exhibit of a selection of his fossils in the Royal Museum. Other specimens are in the *Beginnings* gallery in the Museum of Scotland. Both museums are in Chambers Street. The Hill/Adamson calotypes, including the Miller series, are brought together in 'Nineteenth-Century Scotland in Pictures', a prized collection of the Scottish National Portrait Gallery, 1 Queen Street.

From top: Cromarty Arts Trust interpretive panel at the foot of the South Sutor; Eathie beach; sandstone boulders on the beach

Right: Eathie ravine, where Miller made important finds

Hugh Miller Museum & Birthplace Cottage, Church Street, Cromarty, Ross-shire, IV11 8XA. Tel: 0844 493 2158

While you're in the area …
Within driving distance of the Hugh Miller properties are other attractions managed by the Trust that are well worth visiting:

(1) CULLODEN
Evocative site of the battle that saw the defeat of Bonnie Prince Charlie and the Jacobite cause in 1746. Visitor Centre, restaurant and shop.
Tel: 0844 493 2159

(2) BRODIE CASTLE
Imposing sixteenth-century tower house with a superb art collection and parkland with famous daffodil collection. Tearoom and shop.
Tel: 0844 493 2156

(3) INVEREWE GARDEN
World-famous lochside garden with exotic plants and spectacular views. Visitor Centre, restaurant and shop.
Tel: 0844 493 2225

(4) TORRIDON
Imposing mountains dominate this remote and beautiful countryside, rich in geological and wildlife interest. Ranger guided walks.
Tel: 0844 493 2228

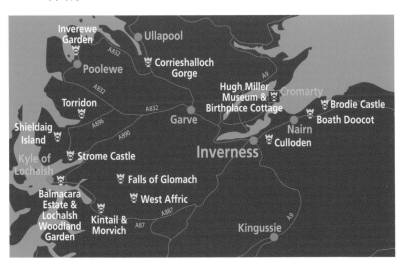

Further reading

The following books by or about Hugh Miller and his period are in print or readily available in libraries.

Books by Hugh Miller

Scenes and Legends of the North of Scotland, B & W Publishing, Edinburgh, 1994, with an introduction by James Robertson

My Schools and Schoolmasters, B & W Publishing, Edinburgh, 1993, with an introduction by James Robertson

The Cruise of the Betsey and *Rambles of a Geologist*, with introduction and additional notes by Michael Taylor, NMS Publishing, Edinburgh, 2003

Testimony of the Rocks, St Matthew Publishing, Cambridge, 2001

Biographies, Critical Studies and a Play

L Borley (ed), *Hugh Miller in Context* (papers of the first two Bicentenary Conferences, The Cromarty Years and the Edinburgh Years), Cromarty Arts Trust, 2002

L Borley (ed), *Celebrating the Life and Times of Hugh Miller: Scotland in the early nineteenth century* (papers of the third Bicentenary Conference), Cromarty Arts Trust, 2003

S Conn, *Hugh Miller, a One-Man Play*, Diehard, Callander, 2002

M Gostwick, *The Legend of Hugh Miller*, Cromarty Courthouse Publications, 1995

M Gostwick, *A Noble Smuggler and Other Stories*, Martin Gostwick, Cromarty, 1997

M A McKenzie Johnston, 'Miller [*née* Fraser], Lydia Mackenzie Falconer (1812-1876)', in H C G Matthew and B Harrison (eds), *Oxford Dictionary of National Biography*, Vol 38, Oxford University Press, 2004 (also www.oxforddnb.com)

G Rosie (ed), *Hugh Miller: Outrage and Order* (selected writings), Mainstream Publishing, Edinburgh, 1981

M A Taylor, 'Miller, Hugh (1802-1856)', in H C G Matthew and B Harrison (eds), *Oxford Dictionary of National Biography*, Vol 38, Oxford University Press, 2004 (also www.oxforddnb.com)

M Shortland (ed), *Hugh Miller's Memoir*, Edinburgh University Press, 1995

S Stevenson, *The Personal Art of David Octavius Hill*, Yale University Press, 2002

E Sutherland, *Lydia, Wife of Hugh Miller of Cromarty*, Tuckwell Press, East Linton, 2002

Access for all

The National Trust for Scotland welcomes disabled visitors to both the Cromarty properties. The following facilities are available in the Hugh Miller Museum:

- Free on-street parking.
- Audio tour of Birthplace Cottage, with ear inductive hooks. (Also available in plain English.)
- Large-print exhibition guide.

The following facilities are available at the Birthplace Cottage:

- Wheelchair access to Courtyard, and Cottage ground floor rooms.
- Audio tour and large-print guide (see above).

The text of this guidebook is available in large print: please contact the Hugh Miller Museum on 0844 493 2158

the National Trust for Scotland
a place for everyone

The National Trust for Scotland for Places of Historic Interest or Natural Beauty is a charity registered in Scotland, Charity No. SC 007410

The National Trust for Scotland is Scotland's leading conservation organisation. It is not a government department, but a charity supported by its membership of over 300,000. Its remit, set out in various Acts of Parliament, is to promote the care and conservation of the Scottish landscape and historic buildings while providing access for the public to enjoy them.

Over 76,000 hectares (187,000 acres) of countryside are in the Trust's care, encompassing magnificent scenery and beautiful gardens. The Trust also owns buildings of historical and architectural importance, from castles to cottages. The future of this heritage depends on you. Please support our valuable work by becoming a member, making a donation or arranging a legacy.